LEADERSHIP

(A Reflection)

Neville A. Stewart

References to the scriptures are taken from the King James Version.
The names used in the personal anecdotes in this publication are fictitious.

Order this book online at www.trafford.com
or email orders@trafford.com

Most Trafford titles are also available at major online book retailers.

Printed in Victoria, BC, Canada.

ISBN: 978-1-4269-2459-0

Library of Congress Control Number: 2009914217

*Our mission is to efficiently provide the world's finest, most
comprehensive book publishing service, enabling every author to
experience success. To find out how to publish your book, your way, and
have it available worldwide, visit us online at www.trafford.com*

Trafford rev. 1/11/10

 www.trafford.com

North America & international
toll-free: 1 888 232 4444 (USA & Canada)
phone: 250 383 6864 ♦ fax: 812 355 4082

In honour of my parents
Hezekiah and Ina Stewart

Table of Contents

Preface

I cannot recall the source, but some time ago I came across the suggestion that a purposeful life is one that has produced children, planted trees and has written at least one book. I have no surviving children, the trees I have planted are few, and this attempt at writing might not qualify as a book.

However it is hoped that by reading it, individuals will not only find it to be a reinforcement of some of their own concepts relating to the subject of leadership but will find some additional useful ideas and approaches to the subject. It is also the hope that readers will be inspired to look with confidence beyond any current personal challenges they might be having.

Acknowledgement

Were it not for my wife's request that I conduct a seminar for one of her church groups on the subject of leadership this project might not have started. Although the seminar never materialised, this book benefited from the ideas that came to mind while I thought about the request.

A special thank you must also be extended to my sister Iona who, when she saw this effort when it was just a few pages, responded in a way that indicated that there was the possibility of it developing into something of worth.

At the completion of chapter 4 when I thought I had said all I wanted to say, I again invited her comments on whether there was any point in seeking to have it published. Her response was an emphatic yes.

I am deeply indebted to the Rev. Dr. Burchell Taylor for his meticulous review of the previous version which has rescued the project from some important pitfalls. I must also express my gratitude for his expression of endorsement for the effort and his suggestions for enhancements.

Chapter 1

Introduction

Scope of the effort

This effort should be viewed as notes reflecting the authors own understanding of the subject based on his work experience both as a leader and as a follower. In these brief comments on the subject of leadership it is taken for granted that at some stage most of us have, or will have assumed the leadership role, no matter how humble. Therefore, most readers will find something here to which they can relate and from which they will be able to draw some inspiration.

In this examination of the subject of leadership an attempt is made at identifying at least some of those attributes which predispose an individual to success as a leader. Consistent with the view that leadership is a job an effort has been made at identifying the critical functions to be fulfilled in executing the role.

One of the views presented in this effort is that on the journey to some leadership roles the road may be characterised by some difficulties. It is suggested that in some instances, despite initial appearances, these difficulties may be orchestrated by a benefactor for the benefit of the individual and or for the benefit of others. Consequently, there is a challenge to bear this in mind when we assess our own experiences or those of others.

It is readily appreciated that by its very nature, leadership entails risks. These risks are many but here, the focus is on those posed by the members of the team or group being led. In the closing chapters an effort is made to identify at least some of the typical set of outcomes to successful leadership.

While no specific audience is targeted, this book should be of interest to those with an interest ·in understanding some of the dynamics which are likely in the leadership experience. It might be of use to those involved in leadership training whether as students or presenters.

Among the themes to which the book subscribes is the idea that God sometimes intervenes in the affairs of men to select some leaders, and through the leadership of these individuals significant changes are made to the course of history. Persons sympathetic to this view will also find something of interest here.

Definition of leadership

"There are almost as many definitions as there are commentators"[1]. However, for the purposes of this reflection, I will define leadership as the ability or skill to guide, direct, or influence others in the pursuit of agreed objectives. The word 'others' is used instead of 'people' because some aspects of the leadership phenomenon are observed in the animal kingdom as well. Note that Leadership skills subsume Management skills[2].

Leadership is successful when agreed objectives are efficiently achieved by the group. In this context, a group may be defined as two or more humans interacting with one another, sharing expectations, obligations and having a common identity. Note that there is no distinction here between "good" and "bad" groups.

Components of leadership

The above definition of leadership implies the presence of a leader and followers in an environment characterised by challenges. The leader is at least expected to offer viable options for meeting these challenges faced by the group. Challenges are many and varied, and are sometimes even frightening. They may include the following:

Colonialism
Racism
Imperialism
Lack of direction
Exploitation
Oppression
Ignorance
Illiteracy
Self contempt
Fear

Superstition
Poverty
Limited resources
Disease
Inadequate infrastructure
High unemployment
Injustice
Nepotism
Corruption
Lack of controls
Lack of accountability

It is readily appreciated that the nature of the environment varies from one leadership situation to another. Typical leadership situations include the home, business departments within an organization or an entire organization, gangs, conglomerates, international organisations, governments and government departments. Accordingly, the size and diversity of the group being led vary with the leadership situations. Diversity within the group that is being led provides opportunities as well as challenges for the leadership process.

Chapter 2

Attributes

The experts speak of leadership traits and list them as Honest, Forward-Looking, Competent, Inspiring and Intelligent[3]. I have a preference for the word attributes, and would suggest that, though not exhaustive, knowledge, understanding, principles, reliability and authority are essential attributes for successful leadership.

knowledge

The importance of this attribute was not lost on Solomon[4]. Adequate and relevant *knowledge* of the environment, the group to be led, and the challenges faced by the group are critical for success. *knowledge* of the environment must provide details on the power brokers involved, the basis of each broker's tenure and influence and the measures employed by each broker to maintain or enhance his or her status and safeguard his or her interest. Many leaders have failed either because of a lack of knowledge in this area or, because of a failure to deal adequately with this reality.

knowledge must include that of the genesis of the challenges being faced by the group. It is clear from the list of possible challenges above that the history and sometimes apparent unassailable nature of some of them require an approach which is informed by specialised knowledge. The various interests served by these challenges must also be known and fully appreciated.

Successful leadership in addition to knowing the membership and its identity must also know the group's expectations and what it sees as its obligations. Every group member has certain expectations of his or her leader. These expectations are based on the perceived capacity of the leader to deliver some improvements to the circumstances of the individual or the group. Group members are often strong on expectations but extremely weak on assuming required obligations. This discrepancy between expectations and obligations on the part of group members often become an additional challenge to be addressed by the leader.

Perhaps one of the most critical *knowledge* component required of effective leadership is that of the relevant weaknesses of each team or group member. Relevant weaknesses of group members could include inadequate technical expertise, health issues or poor communication skills. Generally, where these weaknesses exist, the leadership capacity is severely impaired.

I once had a team member who was technically competent, very co-operative. In fact Harrison was an excellent worker. One day I asked him for a written report on one of the projects on which he was working. A number of days went by and I did not receive the report. As this was uncharacteristic of him, I asked whether he was having a problem. He said no, and promised to let me have it in a day or two. This response however was lacking the usual self confidence for which he was known.

After two days I got the report. I was amazed at the poor quality of the written language, to the extent that I had to ask whether it was actually done by him. The spelling was poor, the grammer and the sentence construction were weak. This young man has always been quite articulate in his speech. Up to this point I was not aware of him having any challenges in the use of the English language. On discussing with him the weaknesses in the written material he confided that he has always had such difficulties in writing.

Harrison's weaknesses in written communication were important because his responsibilities included preparation of user documentation for the products he developed. On becoming aware of his problem I was able to provide coaching and arrange for suitable training courses. More importantly, arrangements were made to ensure that adequate review of his documentation was done before they were released, thereby protecting the image of the department.

understanding

Successful leadership must have an u*nderstanding* of the group's perception of the challenges being faced and the extent to which this perception predisposes the group, not only to seek solutions, but to accept and cooperate with a particular methodology for the attainment of those solutions. As noted above, the history, nature and the scope of the challenges can be many and varied. These must be adequately understood, not only by the leader but must be appreciated by members of the group as well.

The challenges noted above are often the manifestations of systems which have evolved over time. They are sustained by specific agendas, and some times by significant resources. Their techniques and capabilities for survival are usually quite sophisticated. The extent to which this is so must also be understood by the leader, who must then determine whether the group is sufficiently aware of what is being undertaken. So important is this attribute of *understanding* that we have the admonition in the book of Proverbs "Wisdom is the principal thing; therefore get wisdom: and with all thy getting get *understanding*"[5].

vision

For leadership to be successful it must be characterised by a *vision,* not only of the solution, but of the intelligent approach and methodology to be deployed. *vision* is informed and facilitated by *knowledge* and *understanding.* It must be easily communicated and clearly understood by all stakeholders.

"…vision provides direction to the influence process. …… vision, for effectiveness, should allegedly:
- appear as a simple, yet vibrant, image in the mind of the leader

- describe a future state, credible and preferable to the present state
- act as a bridge between the current state and a future optimum state
- appear desirable enough to energize followers"[6]

principles

One of the distinguishing marks of a leader is that he or she is guided by a set of values or *principles* for which he or she is known. In other words, he or she has a public reputation. Interestingly, this is one of the Encarta Dictionary's definitions of character. These principles influence his or her vision, dictate the standard of his or her interactions with others, and circumscribe the methods to which he or she subscribes for the achievement of his or her vision.

It should be noted that *principles* here does not necessarily exclude dishonesty or other undesirable character traits. Recognition of this point assists us in accommodating the view that successful leadership can be sited in the arena of both good and evil endeavours, bearing in mind my above definition of success.

So, as examples of successful leadership we have Moses of the Bible, Martin Luther King Jr., the godfathers of the mafia and the dons of some of our local communities. "Good" Leaders must recognise and appreciate this reality because invariably their mission, of necessity, set them on a collision course with leaderships buoyed by the challenges mentioned above. Fortunately, the perceived success of evil leaderships tends to be short lived.

reliability

A critical attribute of effective leadership is *reliability*. Its manifestations include truthfulness, commitments are faithfully executed and promises are always kept. If and when it becomes impossible to execute commitments and fulfil promises, the situation is promptly admitted and explained. This quality of reliability, along with *principles*, engenders trust not only among the group being led, but among the leader's peers and superiors. *reliability and principles* enhance the motivation process as followers grow to know what to expect of the leader, and consequently, what is expected of them in given situations. They, *reliability and principles* stripped of the undesirable character traits, are the main ingredients of integrity in an individual.

authority

For our purposes, *authority* is the capacity to enforce rules, exact obedience and to secure allegiance to the cause. Leadership without authority is weak. The basis of authority may vary from one leadership environment to another. I noted earlier that a necessary component of the leadership environment is the presence of challenges. To a large extent the leader's *authority* is derived from his capacity or perceived capacity to offer viable options for meeting these challenges. In this regard we note Patrick Jinks' observation, "Direction, protection, and order are the three things humans seek. Authority is given to those who people trust to provide these things"[7].

It is recognised that established leadership positions are endowed with certain authority. A leader coming into such positions is closely observed by all stakeholders to see how he or she exercises this authority and to what end. The new incumbent must quickly assess this authority for relevance and adequacy in relation to his or her vision and mission. This assessment must also include a determination of the mechanism for acquiring or loosing authority. The new leader may find it desirable to secure some modifications to these mechanisms as part of the strategy toward the attainment of the mission.

There are always consequences flowing from the exercise of authority. Successful leaderships examine these consequences for their possible impact on the mission before actually exercising authority. Where an effective examination of the potential consequences is beyond the competence of any one individual, smart leaders are able to identify such instances and then deploy the expertise to effect an adequate evaluation.

Chapter 3

Functions

The job of a leader is to lead. But like any other, the job of leadership must fulfil certain functions. There is still some level of disagreement as to what these are. Any disagreement with the functions suggested in this chapter must take into account the premise established earlier, namely, Leadership skills subsume Management skills.

However, those who would insist on a classification of the relevant business functions into those of Leadership versus those of Management, may be interested in reading an episode of Sanity Savers for IT executives by Jason Hiner entitled "Leadership vs. management: Understand the differences". In my view, the job of successful leadership must embrace the following:

assessment

There is quite an array of issues to be assessed at the start of any leadership endeavour. With an adequate knowledge of the challenges to be addressed, the leader should undertake an *assessment* of the group's perceptions of them. This *assessment* may reveal a lack of consensus on what constitute the challenges. Where there is this lack of agreement, successful leadership proceeds to *assess* the likely impact of the disagreement on the search for solutions. The result of this assessment must be communicated to the group as part of the effort to secure the level of cooperation deemed to be necessary for success.

Another important *assessment* is that of the available resources. Starting with the human resources, a determination is made of the adequacy of the present level and scope of the expertise available in the team or group to be led. Where a deficiency is identified, appropriate steps must be taken to address it. The *assessment* of the human resources is then followed by an *assessment* of other required resources.

The *assessment* process must also include an examination of the possible options to the attainment of the vision, having regard to the nature and scope of the challenge and the level of resources available. The leader then has an obligation and the responsibility to identify the most appropriate option to address the challenge. As noted by M. Kouzes and Barry Z. Posner[8], in this process, the leader experiences and assume risks which implies making mistakes and errors, and suffering failures. Successful leaders accept these as learning opportunities. In this regard, successful leadership must also make allowance for the likely risks resulting from personal initiatives that might be pursued by team members in their effort to support the cause.

planning

Having understood the challenges, done the requisite assessments, and having secured the requisite level of agreement from the group on the identity and scope of the issues, successful leadership develops a *plan* for the way forward. In this exercise the challenges are analysed in detail to determine their cause and the factors sustaining them. The plan must also identify options for solution, the costs/benefits of these solutions, and the time frame for resolution. The planning process must result in a clear vision of not only what is to be achieved but how and when it is going to be achieved and at what cost. The plan must be based on the results of the assessments carried out above and should be realistic.

communication

We may define *communication* as the exchange of thoughts, messages, or information, as by speech, signals, writing, or behaviour. Successful leadership secures the groups acceptance and commitment to the plan for the way forward. This is achieved by a variety of *communication* techniques and strategies, including those in the above definition.

An essential feature of this *communication* however, is that it must provide feedback in both directions. For feedback from the group to be honest and useful, the leader must be perceived to be objective and tolerant of opposing views. In the absence of this perception, feedback will either be nil or lacking in sincerity.

A leader must always be mindful of the potential barriers to effective communication with the group. There is a wide range of sources of "noise" that can interfere with this communication process. In a typical group, communication is impacted by the complex and sometimes conflicting socialising factors or influences of individual members.

Sources of noise affecting the communication process might be classified into two categories, those attributable to the sender and those arising from the receiver of the message. The following are but a few of some of the common sources of noise:

- Language, whether written, spoken or dramatised is an encoding mechanism. If the encoding symbols, in this case words or images, do not have the same interpretation for both sender and receiver the expected outcome of the communication effort will not be achieved. Put another way, both sender and receiver must have a common understanding of the vocabulary employed in the communication process, otherwise misinterpretation will be the result.

- Vocabulary is more than the dictionary's definition (a list of words). Its a list of words with accepted meanings, and meanings can and do change from one context to another. So both sender and receiver must be attuned to the particular context.

- misinterpretation of non-verbal forms of communication is an important source of noise and includes misreading of body language. It is also possible to misread unusual emotional responses to given situations. If an individual is able to perform as part of a choir at the funeral of his or her spouse, is it a reflection of the absence of grief or is a demonstration of commitment to duty?

• Intended outcome to the communication effort can be impacted negatively by the past experiences of the receiver which predisposes him or her to incorrectly anticipate or prejudge the meaning of the message. I recently watched a movie in which an employee was frequently at odds with her boss whom she was always accusing of being unfair to her. However, their project finally ended as a resounding success. In approaching the employee to present her with her final payment, the boss commented that he felt compelled to change the previously agreed figure. Without waiting for an explanation, the employee immediately went into a rage in which she hurled a stream of abuse at the boss. It turned out that the change in the figure was a significant increase.

provider

Execution of the plan to meet the challenges faced by the group invariably requires resources. Therefore in addition to providing direction, protection, and order as mentioned above, the capacity to *provide* and judiciously allocate suitable resources is essential to successful leadership. We observed earlier that, starting with the human resources, a determination must be made of the adequacy of available resources, and that where a deficiency is identified, the leader must take appropriate steps to address such deficiency. To the extent that leaders are seen as *providers*, we may have at least a small part of the explanation for some of the social ills of the modern Jamaican society. This is a society in which a significant number of individuals, in an attempt to address their dissatisfaction with the quantum of their material resources, accept the benevolence of anyone offering to be a provider regardless of the terms and conditions attached. It is this willingness to accept benevolence at any cost that has led to the development of the don man phenomenon and the gang culture in some of our local communities.

Leaders should be aware of the extent to which they are being relied on to provide the required resources for the execution of assigned tasks. In the early years of my teaching career I taught at a school where the desire to participate actively in the interschool athletic championship was quite high but there was no official position of sports master on the staff. I am not known to have any particular enthusiasm for athletics, but having been asked by the principal to do what I could in this area, I co-opted a few of my staff colleagues and mapped out a program.

This program was to be pursued as extracurricular activities. One of the tasks to be accomplished was the marking out of the running track. I assigned this task to John, one of the co-opted staff colleagues and agreed on the afternoon when this work should begin. The marking of the track was one of a number of activities planned for that evening. The various teams turned out and started at their assignments. As part of my monitoring role I was visiting each team to update myself on the progress being made. When I got to John's team nothing had started. I enquired what the problem was. His response was that I had not provided him with a measuring tape so he was just waiting.

I was a bit annoyed because I thought that by virtue of our respective substantive roles in the school, he was better placed to secure a measuring tape than I was. In this situation where we were all expected to be resourceful and enterprising, I felt his posture was unreasonable. As it turned out John's position on the issue was not the result of a lack of resourcefulness but was rather a demonstration of his unspoken disagreement with my being selected to spearhead the program.

The point of this story is that team members can and do often fail to perform and give as an excuse the failure of the leader to provide resources. Leaders should therefore ensure that the responsibility for securing required resources for the execution of assigned tasks is settled early in the game.

Success at the role of provider is often a function of the leader's negotiating skills and the extent of his business and social networking. This is particularly true in situation of scarce resources and contending demands for these scarce resources. Negotiations must take place at a minimum of two levels. Firstly, the leader must negotiate with those from whom the resources must be acquired. Often the challenging items or terms in such negotiations relate to the issues of quantity, delivery schedules, price, and payment schedules. Such negotiations become difficult in situations of high demand and relatively low supply. In such situations the leader is able to bring to bear his knowledge of the possible options and his influence derived from being a member of his network.

Secondly, he must negotiate with the members of his team or group to accept and work with what he has been able to secure on their behalf. This often requires a display of empathy, patience, a willingness to listen and to sincerely examine the demands of team members. The successful leader then presents a response that is properly reasoned, addresses all the issues of the original demand and contains all the relevant justification for the position of the response.

motivation

In terms of the potential for transformation or victory, the relationship between the leader and his followers is like an engine. *motivation* is the fuel of that engine. If members of the group are not fired up into constructive action, leadership is likely to fail although all of the above functions might have been properly executed. In many ways, the motivation process is a selling process. The process is successful when members of the group buy into the idea, project or action being promoted by the leader. *motivation* results in:

- members of the group being fired up into constructive and cooperative action as directed, coached, or delegated depending on the leadership styles being employed. In this constructive and cooperative atmosphere, group members hold each other accountable for the successful performance of their individual roles and are prepared to give assistance to one another if the need arises.

- heightening of the inner driving force of the individual towards attainment of the vision

- encouragement in the face of disappointments

- perseverance despite hardships

- a confidential atmosphere in which the self worth of group members is promoted. A keen sense of self worth or self esteem engenders a commitment to protect that self image by way of high performance and general conduct.

- relevant information is shared resulting in group members feeling empowered and capable.

For these results to be achieved, the leader must get to know and understand each member of the group. Put another way, he must be sufficiently connected to them socially and emotionally in order to transmit the motivational energy appropriately.

The policies and practices which achieve motivation are commonly known and will not be listed here. Instead, we will note the ease with which de-motivation can result, and can sometimes persist for long periods without detection. One of the features of my career is membership of teams at the start up phase of new entities. At one such entity, by the third year of existence, we had earned the reputation of being one of the most efficient public sector organisations. The number of employees was less than forty, but our operations were driven by cutting edge technology managed by the small team I had the honour to lead.

We felt good about the reputation, but one day something happened. It was discovered that a member of my team had for a period of time failed to execute his responsibilities as per the required schedule. The result was that the quality service we were noted for was negatively impacted in at least the experience of the clients directly affected. The consequence to the employee was instant separation from the organisation.

Six months later, the time came for our annual performance evaluation in which "supervisors" evaluate the performance of their team members. My approach to the exercise was to have the team members complete their own assessment which I would then review. I would then have individual meetings with each member in which the final result would be agreed. In these exercises some scores would be decreased while some would be increased. This has always worked well. One of the benefits was the frank exchanges that left each side with an understanding of the other's position on the various items of evaluation. On this occasion however, one member scored herself unusually low. She explained in the review meeting that the separation of the team member earlier in the year left her with a sense of insecurity and consequently, an adverse effect on her sense of commitment to the organisation. She felt that although disciplinary action was required, separation was too drastic an action.

This anecdote suggests a number of lessons. One is the extent to which group members can see their interests inextricably linked to those of their colleagues. But perhaps the most important lesson is the value of having mechanisms for honest feedback on an ongoing basis.

monitoring

Critical to the leadership process is *monitoring* which is an activity or process carried out to ensure that desirable level of success is being achieved against targeted challenges. This involves ensuring that plans are being executed as intended, verifying that resources are adequate and are used optimally; schedules and targets are being met. It also includes determining whether there is a need for modification to the plan in light of new data.

The above anecdote under *motivation* suggests that it would be beneficial to have the *monitoring* process include an ongoing assessment of the motivation level as well. The *monitoring* process should also be concerned with determining whether there is a need to revisit the allocation of responsibilities, or to make adjustments to the span of control of any team member. The process must determine who is accountable for what, and whether the individual deemed to be accountable is aware of this burden and has accepted it and is performing accordingly.

Where the above functions are adequately executed the leader is readily accepted as legitimate. Having achieved this status however, the leader must guard against becoming complacent. He must remain conscious of the fact that group members are always consciously and subconsciously monitoring how rewards and punishment are being administered within the group. There is also an ongoing informal record keeping on who is receiving special favors and for what benefit. An effective leader is expected to be aware of these "reckonings" in order to be sensitive to the group's assessment of his/her enforcement of the rules with respect to the observance of the accepted standard of equity. Where this accepted standard of equity is perceived to be violated with impunity, there is the risk of de-motivation.

Failure to enforce the rules of the group results in members developing a feeling of insecurity, and eventually become easily distracted and agitated. This environment of insecurity, de-motivation, and agitation results in deterioration in the group's performance. Where there is undue delay in addressing this matter, this environment becomes fertile ground for the emergence of challenges for the leadership position.

Chapter 4

Ascent To Leadership

Individuals come into leadership in response to circumstances at the time. Circumstances may be characterised by:

- miscarried cruelty
- the agenda of the prospective leader's benefactor.
- characteristics of the local and or international environment
- coincidence of the need for leadership and the presence of an individual with the required qualifications

These circumstances are not necessarily mutually exclusive. An individual might very well be able to identify in his own experience a combination of elements from two or more of these circumstances.

Miscarried Cruelty

Many, on the journey to becoming leaders, travel a road which is the result of the cruelty of others. We may look at the life of Joseph as dramatised in the book of Genesis as an example of this. Joseph, the youngest of the sons of Jacob was his father's favourite. This fact along with what was regarded as some prophetic utterances about their future relative status resulted in his brothers' hatred for him.

In chapter 37 we read "And when his brethren saw that their father loved him more than all his brethren, they hated him" [9]. Such was the intensity of the hatred that as soon as it became convenient they said "Come now therefore, and let us slay him, and cast him into some pit, and we will say, some evil beast hath devoured him"[10]. One of the brothers succeeded in convincing the others to moderate this plan to destroy Joseph. Joseph was therefore put into the pit unharmed[11].

This act of cruelty was further modified at the suggestion of another brother who reasoned that it was more profitable to sell Joseph than to leave him in the pit. So "…they drew and lifted up Joseph out of the pit, and sold Joseph to the Ishme-el-ites for twenty pieces of silver: and they brought Joseph into Egypt"[12] Joseph on arrival in Egypt was again sold to Potiphar, an officer of the king Pharaoh.

Joseph's brothers no doubt were now satisfied that by their acts of cruelty, they had at last done away with their brother permanently. However the story informs that Joseph in his new environment in Egypt was now a prosperous man[13] The scheme to destroy him has suffered a miscarriage. Instead of destruction there was prosperity and an elevated status.

On the basis of this prosperity and the perceived source of it, Joseph was elevated to be fully in charge of his master's estate[14]. This was to be but the beginning of an extraordinary leadership career. In this career he planned for, and successfully managed a seven year period of famine throughout the land of Egypt. We note that one benefit of this leadership was the provision for the survival from the famine, of those brothers who were so cruel to him.

Among the many lessons to be learnt from the story is the importance of the proper assessment of our experiences, particularly our good fortunes. Joseph's brothers expected and feared his revenge for their cruelty against him. Joseph however was not only quick to assure them of his forgiveness but made the point that "....ye thought evil against me; but God meant it unto good, to bring to pass, as it is this day, to save much people alive."[15]

In the event that you think you are currently the victim of some act of *cruelty* perpetrated by others, be encouraged that chances are, the outcome will be a miscarriage of the cruelty which will result in not only honour and prosperity, but a higher calling.

Benefactor's Agenda

Some leaders' ascent to the role is not so much by their own desire or engineering but by the orchestrations of their benefactor. We will look at another example from the Old Testament.

In the book of Exodus we have the dramatic story of how Moses came to be the leader of the children of Israel. The children of Israel were in the midst of a major challenge. They had become slaves to the Egyptians and have been crying out to God for deliverance. God, Moses' benefactor, having selected him, appeared to him via an angel in the burning bush and appointed him as the one to "bring forth my people the children of Israel out of Egypt"[16].

We note Moses' immediate response. He tries to decline the proposal as if it were an offer, pointing to his inadequacy first by asking "Who am I, that I should go to Pharaoh, and that I should bring forth the children of Israel out of Egypt"[17]. The question Who am I? is pointing to Moses' feeling of inferiority when he compares his perceived social and political status with that of Pharaoh. This issue of inferiority complex has often undermined our individual potential for significant achievement in our sphere of leadership.

Having received God's response to his first claim of inadequacy, Moses raises the issue of his authority as another area of inadequacy by asking "what shall I say" when they ask me the name of him who sent me? It is interesting that this question is being posed even after God "said Certainly I will be with thee"[18]. God's response to Moses' second claim of inadequacy was quite elaborate. It included what Moses should say that would cause his audience to recall God's action on their behalf in the past.

But despite this elaborate response of God to Moses' protestations, Moses continues to plea inadequacy, pointing to a third issue, "I am not eloquent, …………..but I am slow of speech, and of a slow tongue"[19]. Understandably, we read that by this time God became angry with Moses. These exchanges between God and Moses arose from a clear conflict of their agendas.

Probably, Moses' resistance arising from his sense of inadequacy would have been much less, had he been more appreciative of his personal history. This history includes the circumstances which led to his being placed in the bulrushes as a baby, his rescue by the daughter of the arch enemy of his people, and becoming the son of the said daughter, and his eventual return to his own people. An appreciation of this personal history would have facilitated the recognition of an agenda culminating in this commissioning encounter with God his benefactor.

Perhaps there is a message here for all of us. It is important to reflect on our personal history periodically, particularly when confronted by puzzling challenges. Permit a brief personal story to illustrate the point. In my career I have had the fortune of holding a number of CIO (Chief Information Officer) positions. In these positions I usually structure my area of responsibility into three functional units, each headed by a unit manager. An important feature of my leadership style is a focus on continuity, so that the operation should never suffer from the absence of anyone, including myself.

After a three year period in one of these CIO positions, my CEO (Chief Executive Officer) called me on the phone and instructed that I should hand over to one of my unit managers as I was being separated from the company. Up to this point I thought I enjoyed not only the confidence but the loyalty of this gentleman. I was one of three members of the layer below him. I was the one who acted for him in his absence. So this unexpected and hostile directive was puzzling indeed.

Fortunately for me, I have an unusual attitude to possessions, including jobs. I don't see them as indispensible to my existence. Perhaps this is as a result of my humble background and the struggles involved in moving from that background to that associated with being a CIO, or maybe I have been influenced by the story of Job.

I proceeded with the handing over process without any questions until a few days later. My actual question to the CEO was "How did we get here?" His answer was that there was a need to rationalise the operations. I did not buy this response but I left the discussion at that, and provided myself with a few possible reasons based on my sense of the politics in the organisation at the time.

The separation was not immediate, so I decided to access the benefit of my health card before I turned it in, by going for a general medical examination, although I did not expect any unfavourable outcome. At age 58, the only ailments I was aware of were the occasional bouts of the flue and the need to wear eye glasses. I had recently participated in a sprint race at our Fun Day and finished ahead of a 21 year old.

As part of the medical examination, my doctor decided to include the PSA test (a test for prostate cancer). I got the test results subsequent to the separation date. These results indicated that I had prostate cancer. Further test showed that the diagnosis was made in time to avoid the usual swift and fatal outcome which is usually associated with this disease.

I have always reflected on my personal history periodically. At 65, I find I do so more frequently, and when I do, this episode always stands out as an important item in what I consider to be my benefactor's agenda. I now view the CEO's action as one that was completely out of his control. Without realising it, he acted as an agent of my benefactor. That action, in addition to possibly facilitating an extension of my life resulted in my securing eventually a significantly better CIO position.

Where the reflection on ones personal history results in ones recognition of a benefactor's intervention on ones behalf, there are a number of outcomes. Firstly, there is a sense of gratitude to the benefactor. A feature of this sense of gratitude is a feeling of indebtedness, particularly when the outcome of the intervention exceeds ones own capabilities. Secondly there is a sense of support and empowerment in the face of difficulties. This sense of gratitude is often accompanied by a heighten awareness of ones own vulnerability. Thirdly, it informs ones interactions with others as one recognises the possibility that the benefactor could be acting on their behalf as well. When God is the benefactor, these observations have some awesome implications.

In addition to demonstrating the fact that there are leadership episodes in which the leader emerged at the dictates and manoeuvrings of a benefactor instead of those of his own, the Moses example also illustrates some of the self doubts that some leaders have to overcome. The following extract suggests that even the great George Washington had his experience of self doubts:

> *"Mount Vernon, April 1, 1789.*

.... my movements to the chair of Government will be accompanied by feelings not unlike those of a culprit who is going to the place of his execution: so unwilling am I, in the evening of a life nearly consumed in public cares, to quit a peaceful abode for an Ocean of difficulties, without that competency of political skill, abilities and inclination which is necessary to manage the helm. I am sensible, that I am embarking on the voice of my Countrymen and a good name of my own, on this voyage, but what returns will be made for them, Heaven alone can foretell"[20].

The Local and International Environment

It could be argued that the ascent of some leaders result directly from the characteristics of the local and or international environment at the time. We will take Michael Manley as our example of this case. Manley, having secured the leadership of the Jamaican government, was to become later an influential figure in the international scene. The following extract from Wikipedia summarizes Manley's strategy in exploiting the political climate of his time on his way to becoming an international leader "Manley developed close friendships with several foreign leaders, foremost of whom were Julius Nyerere of Tanzania, Olof Palme of Sweden, Pierre Trudeau of Canada and Fidel Castro of Cuba. With Cuba just 145 km (90 miles) north of Jamaica, he strengthened diplomatic relations between the two island nations, much to the dismay of United States policymakers.

At the 1979 meeting of the Non-Aligned Movement, Manley strongly pressed for the development of what was called a natural alliance between the Non-aligned movement and the Soviet Union to battle imperialism. In his speech he said, "All anti-imperialists know that the balance of forces in the world shifted irrevocably in 1917 when there was a movement and a man in the October Revolution, and Lenin was the man." Manley saw Cuba and the Cuban model as having much to offer both Jamaica and the world.

In diplomatic affairs, Manley believed in respecting the different systems of government of other countries and not interfering in their internal affairs"[21].

Undoubtedly Manley's success was due in no small measure to his personal attributes and expertise but the contribution and facilitation of the international mood of the period, influenced by his friends who were of like minds must be acknowledged. The view that ascent to some leadership is facilitated by the current social and political environment is not new and was recognised by Shakespeare when he observed:

"There is a tide in the affairs of men.
Which, taken at the flood, leads on to fortune;"[24]

Coincidence of Need and Qualified Individual

Perhaps the most common circumstance resulting in the ascent to leadership is the coincidence of a need for a leader and the presence of an individual with the required qualification. This tends to be the case in organisations where sufficient attention has been paid to succession planning.

Wikipedia summarizes the principle of Succession planning as follows:

"Succession planning is the process of identifying and preparing suitable employees through mentoring, training and job rotation, to replace key players — such as the chief executive officer (CEO) — within an organization as their terms expire. From the risk management aspect, provisions are made in case no suitable internal candidates are available to replace the loss of any key person. It is usual for an organization to insure the key person so that funds are available if she or he dies and these funds can be used by the business to cope with the problems before a suitable replacement is found or developed.

Succession Planning involves having senior executives periodically review their top executives and those in the next lower level to determine several backups for each senior position. This is important because it often takes years of grooming to develop effective senior managers. ....

A careful and considered plan of action ensures that the least possible disruption to the person's responsibilities and therefore the organization's effectiveness. Examples include such a person who is

- suddenly and unexpectedly unable or unwilling to continue their role within the organization;
- accepting an approach from another organization or external opportunity which will terminate or lessen their value to the current organization;
- indicating the conclusion of a contract or time-limited project; or
- moving to another position and different set of responsibilities within the organization.

A succession plan clearly sets out the factors to be taken into account and the process to be followed in relation to retaining or replacing the person."[22] Succession planning is one of the important issues to be addressed by successful leaderships. It is critical to ensuring the continuity of the enterprise.

Chapter 5

Risks Occasioned By the Team

In chapter 3, we made the point that successful leadership must also make allowance for the likely risks resulting from personal initiatives that might be pursued by team members. In this chapter we look a little closer at this issue.

For the purposes of this discussion I will define Risk as the possibility of an undesirable outcome. Leadership is sometimes put at risk as a result of the actions or utterances of members of the team or group. Such actions and utterances are often the result of overzealousness or ignorance of the leader's agenda rather than a desire to be malicious. The genesis of such zeal is often times the genuine desire on the part of the member to demonstrate loyalty to the leader and the cause or to be recognised as a star performer.

Overzealous Loyalty

While loyalty to the leader and the cause is highly desirable, it becomes a liability when it loses objectivity, misinterprets or misrepresents the leader's vision. Of course this phenomenon is not new. Jesus not only knew his mission on earth but he also had a clear vision of how this mission was going to be fulfilled. In the gospel of St. John[23] we have an account of how he was arrested. He knew and accepted that this event was all a part of the mission, but his team member Peter, in an act of zealous defence of the leader, resorted to the use of his sword which resulted in the high priest's servant loosing his right ear. Jesus in reprimanding Peter made the point that such action was not consistent with the mission. It is required of successful leaders that they be always aware of the potential risks of team member acting counter to the vision, even though it might be out of a spirit of loyalty and enthusiasm.

Overzealous Performance

The zeal to acquire the reputation as a star performer often presents with the temptation to ignore established procedures and rule. This trait is also sometimes characterised by a level of arrogance. While the star performer can be a significant asset to the mission of the leadership, unbridled zeal in this area can be an embarrassment to the leader and a risk to the cause.

In my third job in the Information and Communication Technology (ICT) industry, I was part of a team charged with the responsibility of converting the organisation's operations from a manual system to a computerised one.

As a result of my contribution to the success of the conversion of the first application I was promoted to my first supervisory role in the industry and given the responsibility to lead the conversion process of the next application. I recruited Ronald, a young bright computer programmer as a member of the team to undertake this project. In the interview there was some emphasis on the fact that there was a time constraint on the project, but Ronald was quite confident that he was equal to the challenge.

The approach and methodology for the project were outlined and agreed. As part of this methodology Ronald was asked to document the requirements of the new system. This he did. I reviewed the document and pointed out some needed modifications. In my estimation the initial development work should take at least two weeks. After a week and a half as I entered my office that morning I was greeted by a beaming Ronald who announced that 'the new system was implemented last night'.

His glee and excitement were short lived and disappointment set in when I asked:

What do you mean by implemented?

Did I see the revised documentation?

When was the system tested?

Has the user manual been developed and approved?

Did you secure a signed off user acceptance of the system?

Of course the answers to these questions were in the negative. Ronald thought that the urgency of getting the new system in place justified ignoring these procedures. Naturally, the system manifested some serious defects and had to be deactivated later that day. As a consequence my leadership of the project came in for some criticism from senior management. However valuable lessons were learnt by all and these lessons served us well in the management of subsequent development work.

Leaders must always be cognisant of the possibility of followers/team members being overcome by the desire to be seen as star performers and implement mechanisms to minimise this threat. Such mechanisms might include predetermined sanctions which have been adequately communicated.

Ignorance of the Leader's Agenda

A leader may be at risk by the team member pursuing an otherwise normal agenda but an agenda which is not in sync with that of the leader. I got caught in such a situation once. I was recruited to work on a project that was started some years before. My mandate was to evaluate the documentation done previously and to prepare a technical proposal for the implementation of the project.

I was convinced that I was given this assignment because of my reputation for succeeding at these types of projects. Consequently, with a sense of obligation to this reputation I pursued the task with urgency. The preparation and submission of monthly progress reports was an important part of the culture of this organisation. Supervisors at one level compiled reports to their supervisors from the reports submitted by their team members.

I was determined that my first monthly report should create a favourable impression, and it did. However by the third report in which time frames for the various phases of the project were being proposed, I began to sense some hostility from my team leader about the contents of the report. Some activities listed as completed were arbitrarily dismissed as needing additional effort, efforts which to my mind did not add any significant value to the project.

Then came the report of the fourth month which indicated that my assignment was almost complete. My team leader was not at all amused. He wanted to know what he would have to report on the next month if I conveyed the impression that my work was done. It finally dawned on me that his agenda was not to have the project completed, but instead the objective was to ensure that he could always report that something was being done.

This experience demonstrates at least two points. The first is that some leaders can be dishonest in the execution of their responsibilities. As is the case most times, dishonesty may result from insecurity, born of a fear that we will not be able to face the consequences when our inadequacies are revealed. Perhaps in this case the real reason might have been slothfulness, not wanting to have to take on a new endeavour.

The second point is that, as mentioned in Chapter 2, the leadership attributes do not necessarily include honesty. By the measure of longevity in the position this supervisor could be said to have had a successful tenure. Of course, the fact that he got away with this approach to his responsibilities, indicates that a serious deficiency existed in the leadership function of his then supervisor. Leaders must always be on the alert for attempts at this kind of deception from team members. This anecdote does emphasize not only the need for the monitoring function, but indicates this function must be executed in a manner that renders it effective in detecting such dishonesty.

Chapter 6

Outcomes of Successful Leadership

At the end of a successful leadership we are inevitably left with a number of outcomes. The outcomes considered here are messages, images, and changes.

Messages

Here I am using one of the Encarta Dictionary's meaning of message, "a lesson, moral, or important idea communicated, e.g. in a work of art". Such messages when taken together provide at least a summary of the mission undertaken by the leadership and highlight those features which command attention. These messages speak to the following:

- ### *Mission*

There is a message which defines the mission which was achieved or still to be accomplished. It resonates with at least some members of the community and motivates them into becoming sympathisers or active supporters. For these sympathisers and supporters, this message of the mission provides hope and inspiration for the future. On the other hand it might spell doom for the stakeholders of the challenge being targeted by the mission.

• *Challenges*

Usually, a mission is about overcoming challenges. Therefore, there is a message identifying the relevant challenges. For this message to be clear, the source or sources and or the cause or causes of the challenges are precisely defined. Invariably, in addressing challenges there are interests that will feel threatened. Consequently, in identifying the challenges the possible responses to the perceived threat are included. This message, in defining the relevant challenges, result in a heightened awareness in the community. This heightened awareness increases the potential for action for and against the mission.

• *Process*

The achievement of a successful mission is the result of a systematic process. Whether by pronouncement or demonstration, there is a message outlining this process. This message identifies the players and their roles and addresses how these roles are coordinated according to an agreed agenda. The required resources and the viable options for securing them are articulated. An accurate message outlining the process might also indicate pitfalls encountered and how they were addressed.

- ### *Victories*

For the leadership to be classified as successful there must be messages of triumphs. These messages not only indicate the challenges successfully met, but how they were actually met and at what cost and at what sacrifice. At least some of the beneficiaries and potential beneficiaries are identified.

- ### *Failures*

In real life, we have to admit that at least some of the times, even where the leadership is declared successful, there are aspects of the mission that are disappointing. This should not be surprising since it was observed in chapter 3 that risks and disappointments are inherent in leadership. Messages of failure can therefore be expected. If and when these messages are presented, they should be examined for the useful lessons they contain with a view to benefitting from these lessons in the future.

Images

The second outcome of a successful leadership is a set of images, chief of which is the image of the leader. The significant contributors to this image are the messages discussed above. The examination of any successful leadership on the basis of these messages inevitably leaves the audience with a mental image of the leader.

An interesting point here is the fact that in many instances this image is the same for the majority of the audience. It is this image which inspires in the audience certain emotions towards the leader. These include respect or contempt, love or hate, trust or suspicion. Of course it is recognised that the actual emotion from any given member of the audience will be influence by that member's own value system, socialisation and his or her own vested interest and the extent to which these interest have been impacted by the leadership.

The messages also generate images of the environment, before, during and after the leadership regime. These images of the environment are likely to include those of the various stakeholders and their contribution for or against the leader and the leadership process. These images facilitate a comparison between the current and previous state. These messages and images can sometimes evoke very strong emotions for or against the leadership.

Changes

Thirdly, there is the outcome of change. Among the changes will be the results of the challenges overcome. Consequently the community or at least some members of the community benefit directly. Such benefits might even extend to posterity.

Supporters or sympathisers would have been won. These may be persons who have benefitted directly or indirectly from the results of the mission. They might be individuals who are sufficiently enlighten to recognise that though they might not have benefitted directly in any tangible way, the fact that the community benefitted, the mission is deserving of their support. On the other hand, it is quite likely that detractors would emerge as well. These could include those whose interests were the direct or indirect targets of the mission, and who must now adapt to the new realities resulting from the achievements of the mission. This particular dual outcome usually sets the stage for a continuation of the mission, albeit under new leadership.

Perhaps the most significant of the changes are those concerning the team being lead. Members of the team would have undergone some improvements in their knowledge base as a result of their own involvement and contribution to the leadership process. Some would have had a modification in their attitudes to some of the issues encountered. The confidence levels of most team members would also be positively impacted. With these outcomes on the team, members are likely to continue to have an impact on the community even though the particular leadership regime might have formally come to an end.

In looking at the changes concerning the team, let us not ignore the possibility that a minority of members might experience a sense of disillusionment. This is likely where there was dissonance on specific details of the mission as perceived by such members. Some of the disillusioned might even become part of the detractors mentioned above. Sometimes the outcomes include the start of new entities with leaders who were former members of the previous leadership. These new leaders may emerge either from those whose confidence levels have been positively impacted or from the disillusioned.

Chapter 7

Conclusion

We may, or should conclude that the leadership role is an opportunity. Here my choice of meaning of opportunity is the Encarta Dictionary's rendition "a combination of favourable circumstances or situations". As such it should be pursued and executed responsibly, bearing in mind:

- The need for a set of appropriate attributes all of which might not be present at the outset. Smart leaders therefore seek to address these deficiencies as early as possible after ascension to the role. Where appropriate, specialised expertise should be acquired and applied in securing an adequate knowledge base and understanding of the challenges to be faced.
- It's a job, requiring ongoing attention to the relevant functions, chief of which are strategic planning, adequate monitoring and effective communication.

- The combination of favourable circumstances or situations might not be entirely of the leader's own making and therefore when this is so he has a benefactor. The recognition of the existence of a benefactor should inform or influence ones interactions with others as one recognises the possibility that the same benefactor could be acting on their behalf as well. It is smart to strive to be in sync with ones benefactor's agenda.
- There are risks which must be recognised and catered for. A significant source of risks is the team or group being led. The risks from this source tend to arise more from overzealousness than from malice. None the less, appropriate mechanism should be implemented to minimise this threat.
- The outcomes of a particular leadership include changes to the lives of others which can continue to affect the community long after the tenure of that leadership. This should therefore inform the choices made in executing the role.

References

1. Doyle, M. E. and Smith, M. K. (2001) 'Classical leadership', *the encyclopedia of informal education*, http://www.infed.org/leadership/traditional_leadership.htm
2. Leadership 501 Leadership vs. Management November 7, 2006
3. from Kouzes and Posner's research into leadership that was done for the book *The Leadership Challenge*. (Leadership 501)
4. 2Chronicles 1: 9-10
5. Proverbs 4:7
6. Wikipedia, the free encyclopedia - Theories of leadership
7. Patrick Jinks. Leadership vs. Authority. 2007 SLC Blog: May 18, 2007
8. Summary from the book The Leadership Challenge by James M. Kouzes and Barry Z. Posner
9. Genesis 37:4
10. Genesis 37: 20
11. Genesis 37:21-24
12. Genesis 37:28
13. Genesis 39:2
14. Genesis 39:5-6
15. Genesis 50:20
16. Exodus 3:10
17. Exodus 3:11
18. Exodus 3:12
19. Exodus 4:10

20. The Writings of George Washington from the Original Manuscript Sources, 1745-1799. John C. Fitzpatrick, Editor.--vol. 30
21. Wikipedia, the free encyclopedia - Michael Manley
22. Wikipedia, the free encyclopedia Succession planning
23. St. John 18:10-11.
24. William Shakespeare Julius Caesar Act 4, scene 3, 218–224.